Young Animals

Rachel Bladon

OXFORD
UNIVERSITY PRESS

OXFORD
UNIVERSITY PRESS

Great Clarendon Street, Oxford, OX2 6DP, United Kingdom

Oxford University Press is a department of the University of Oxford. It furthers the University's objective of excellence in research, scholarship, and education by publishing worldwide. Oxford is a registered trade mark of Oxford University Press in the UK and in certain other countries

ISBN: 978 0 19 464633 8

An Audio CD Pack containing this book and a CD is also available, ISBN 978 0 19 464643 7

The CD has a choice of American and British English recordings of the complete text.

An accompanying Activity Book is also available, ISBN 978 0 19 464654 3

Printed in China

This book is printed on paper from certified and well-managed sources.

ACKNOWLEDGEMENTS

Illustration by: Kelly Kenney pp.10, 16; Alan Rowe pp.21, 23, 24, 27, 30, 31.

The publisher would like to thank the following for their kind permission to reproduce photographs and other copyright material: Alamy Images pp.4 (Chick hatching/Christopher Taylor), 7 (Loggerhead turtles hatching/Mark Conlin), 11 (Swell shark/ Mark Conlin), 12 (Harp seal with pup/Keren Su/China Span), 15 (Beaver/Wildlife), 19 (Beetle larva/Nigel Cattlin), 19 (Bark beetle/Nigel Cattlin); Corbis pp.10 (Grey Kangaroo with joey/ Frans Lanting), 11 (Silk moth caterpillar/Thomas Marent/ Minden Pictures), 13 (Great gray owl feeding chick/Tom Vezo/ Minden Pictures), 16 (Bald eagle with offspring/Yva Momatiuk & John Eastcott/Minden Pictures), 19 (Bark beetle pupa/Nigel Cattlin/Visuals Unlimited); FLPA pp.5 (Zebra with foal/Elliott Neep), 14 (Brown bear with cubs/Gerard Lacz), 18 (Lion pride/ Ariadne Van Zandbergen); Getty Images pp.3 (Elephant with calf/Michael Poliza), 6 (Caterpillar/Don Johnston), 8 (Elephant with calf/Michael Poliza), 13 (Common toad/Ian West), 15 (Beaver dam/Danita Delimont); Nature Picture Library pp.6 (Seahorse gives birth/Alex Mustard), 9 (Chimpanzees/ Anup Shah), 9 (Ostrich pair with chicks/Vincent Munier), 13 (Toad tadpole with back legs/Fabio Liverani), 17 (Cheetah family/Anup Shah); Oxford University Press pp.3 (Mallard ducklings/Photodisc), 3 (Kitten/Corbis/Digital Stock), 3 (Tadpoles/Thinkstock), 6 (Butterfly/Purestock).

Introduction

Young animals grow up from babies into adults. Some young animals grow up very fast. Some young animals grow up slowly.

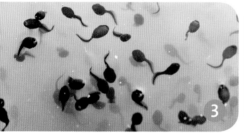

What are these young animals?
What young animals do you like?

Now read and discover more about young animals!

Babies

Some babies hatch from an egg.

A mother duck makes a nest by the water. She lays her eggs in the nest. She sits on the eggs so they stay warm. Then the ducklings hatch.

A Duckling

egg

nest

Some babies don't hatch from an egg. They are born from their mother.

A baby zebra is born from its mother. The mother cleans the baby and then it can stand up and walk. It can run when it's one hour old!

A Zebra and Its Baby

stripes

Discover!

A baby zebra has brown and white stripes.

Go to page 20 for activities.

2 Parents

Many young animals look the same as their parents. Look at these baby seahorses and their parent.

Some young animals look very different from their parents. A caterpillar is a butterfly's baby.

Seahorses

baby

parent

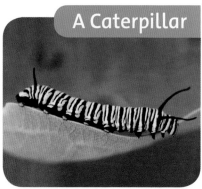

A Caterpillar

A Butterfly

Some young animals live with their parents for weeks. Some young animals live with their parents for years. Parents feed and protect their babies.

Some young animals don't meet their parents! A mother sea turtle lays her eggs in the sand. Then she goes into the ocean. Baby sea turtles hatch from the eggs. They don't meet their mother.

Baby Sea Turtles

Go to page 21 for activities.

 Help

Many adult animals help young animals.

A young elephant lives with its mother and other elephants. The mother feeds the young elephant. She cleans it, and she gives it water. Adult elephants protect the young elephant. They help it to walk, too!

Elephants

Chimpanzees

A mother chimpanzee carries her babies everywhere.

Ostriches

A young ostrich lives with its mother and father. They help it to feed. They also protect it from the rain and the hot sun with their wings.

wing

Go to page 22 for activities.

4 Danger

pouch

A Kangaroo and Its Baby

There's danger for young animals.
Other animals want to eat them.
How do young animals stay safe?

Young kangaroos live in their
mother's pouch. It's safe there.

Discover!

Baby kangaroos are very
little. You can put a baby
kangaroo on a spoon!

spots

ocean floor

A Young Shark

This young shark has spots. Other animals can't see the shark on the ocean floor.

This caterpillar has poison in its body. Other animals touch the caterpillar, and poison goes into them.

A Caterpillar

Go to page 23 for activities.

5 Food

Some young animals drink milk from their mother. The milk is good and it helps them to grow. A young seal drinks its mother's milk.

Seals

Discover!

A young seal can grow from 10 kilograms to 30 kilograms in three weeks!

A young owl doesn't drink milk. Its parents feed it frogs, fish, and other little animals.

A toad eats insects and other little animals. A baby toad is very different. A baby toad is called a tadpole and it eats plants.

A Toad

A Tadpole

Go to page 24 for activities.

13

Young bears are born when the weather is very cold. The mother makes a home called a den. She puts branches and grass in an old tree or under a rock. The young bears are warm in the den, and they're safe from other animals.

A Bear's Den

Beavers make a home called a lodge. They cut down trees and branches, and they make a dam in a river. The beavers make a lodge in the water, with branches and mud. A young beaver is safe in the lodge.

beaver

lodge

dam

river

Go to page 25 for activities.

How Animals Learn

Young animals learn many things. A young eagle learns to fly when it's about ten weeks old. The parents help the young eagle to fly.

Eagles

Cheetahs

Young cheetahs watch their mother hunt. This helps them to learn to hunt. The mother cheetah gives little animals to her young cheetahs, too. The young cheetahs learn how to hunt and eat the little animals.

A cheetah can run more than 100 kilometers per hour. That's very, very fast!

→ Go to page 26 for activities.

How Animals Grow Up

A young lion lives with its mother and other lions in a pride. When it's about two years old, a young male lion moves to a different pride.

A Pride of Lions

A young beetle is called a larva. The larva looks very different from its parents. It grows a pupa. When it comes out of the pupa, it's an adult. Then it looks the same as its parents.

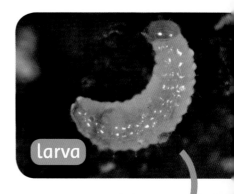

larva

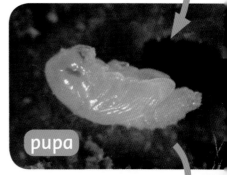

pupa

adult beetle

Young animals grow up into adults and have babies. Their babies have babies, too. Every day, young animals are born!

→ Go to page 27 for activities.

1 Babies

← Read pages 4–5.

1 **Complete the sentences. Then write the numbers.**

eggs ~~nest~~ hatch warm

1 A duck makes a ___nest___ .

2 A duck lays her _____ in a nest.

3 A duck sits on her eggs so they stay _____.

4 Ducklings _____ in a nest.

2 **Circle the correct words.**

1 A zebra **hatches** / **doesn't hatch** from an egg.

2 A baby zebra has **black** / **brown** and white stripes.

3 A baby zebra can run when it's one **minute** / **hour** old.

② Parents

← Read pages 6–7.

caterpillar ~~sea turtle~~
seahorse butterfly

1 Write the words.

1   _sea turtle_

2   _____

3   _____

4   _____

2 Write *true* or *false*.

1 A baby seahorse looks the same
  as its parents.   _true_

2 A caterpillar looks the same
  as its parents.   _____

3 Some animals live with their
  parents for weeks.   _____

4 A mother sea turtle lays her eggs
  in the ocean.   _____

③ Help

← Read pages 8–9.

1 Match.

1 It lives with its mother and other adults.

2 Its parents protect it with their wings.

3 Its mother carries it everywhere.

an ostrich
an elephant
a chimpanzee

2 Answer the questions.

1 Who feeds a young elephant?
   A mother elephant feeds a young elephant.

2 Who helps a young elephant to walk?
   _____

3 Who carries a baby chimpanzee?
   _____

4 Who lives with a young ostrich?
   _____

4 Danger

← Read pages 10–11.

1 Complete the puzzle. Then find the secret word.

1 →	s	p	o	t	s

2 →

3 →

4 →

5 →

6 →

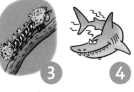

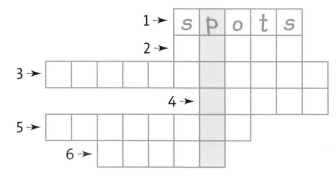

The secret word is:

2 Circle the correct words.

1 Some animals **live** / **eat** young animals.

2 Young **kangaroos** / **caterpillars** live in their mother's pouch.

3 You can put a baby **shark** / **kangaroo** on a spoon.

4 Some caterpillars have **poison** / **sharks** in their body.

5 Food

← Read pages 12–13.

tadpole   seal
owl   toad

1   Write the words.

1 _____

2 _____

3 _____

4 _____

2   Write *true* or *false*.

1   Some young animals drink
   milk from their mother.   _____

2   A young seal can grow from
   10 kilograms to 30 kilograms
   in three days.   _____

3   A young owl drinks its mother's milk.   _____

4   A tadpole eats insects and other
   little animals.   _____

6 Homes

← Read pages 14–15.

1 Find and write the words.

a	o	b	e	a	r	r
b	e	b	s	n	c	h
b	e	a	v	e	r	o
r	b	r	a	n	c	h
n	h	c	i	o	k	s
g	r	a	s	s	m	y
b	r	s	s	c	h	s

1 <u>bear</u>   2 <u>b</u>

3 <u>g</u>   4 <u>b</u>

2 Complete the sentences.

mud   den   dam   lodge

1 A mother bear makes a home called a _____.

2 Beavers make a home called a _____.

3 Beavers make a _____ in a river.

4 Beavers make their home with branches
   and _____.

7 How Animals Learn

← Read pages 16–17.

1 Write the words.

fly   run   eat   hunt

1 _____

2 _____

3 _____

4 _____

2 Match.

1 Young cheetahs
2 A mother cheetah
3 A young eagle

learns to fly when it's about ten weeks old.

gives little animals to her young cheetahs.

watch their mother hunt.

8 How Animals Grow Up

← Read pages 18–19.

1 Write the words. Then match.

1 n o l i

___lion___

2 v r a a l

_____

3 u a p p

_____

4 e b e l e t

_____

2 Complete the sentences.

larva   adult   pride   pupa

1 A young lion lives in a _____.

2 A young beetle is called a _____.

3 A larva grows a _____.

4 When a larva comes out of a pupa it's an

_____.

Young Animals

1 Choose a young animal. Answer the questions.

Young animal: _____

Does it hatch from an egg? ☐ Yes ☐ No

Does it look the same
as its parents? ☐ Yes ☐ No

Does it live with its parents? ☐ Yes ☐ No

How does it stay safe? _____

What does it eat? _____

Where does it live? _____

How does it learn? _____

_____

2 Draw or find a picture of a young animal. Then complete the sentences.

This is a _____ .

It looks _____ .

It _____ from an egg.

It _____ with its parents.

To stay safe, it _____

It eats _____

It lives _____

To learn, it _____

Picture Dictionary

 adult

 animals

 born

 branches

 clean

 cut down

 danger

 different

 eggs

 fast

 food

 grass

 grow up

 hatch

 hour

 hunt

insects

lay

male

mud

nest

ocean

parents

plants

poison

protect

rock

safe

same

sand

slowly

warm

Oxford Read and Discover

Series Editor: Hazel Geatches • CLIL Adviser: John Clegg

Oxford Read and Discover graded readers are at six levels, for students from age 6 and older. They cover many topics within three subject areas, and support English across the curriculum, or Content and Language Integrated Learning (CLIL).

Available for each reader:
- Audio CD Pack (book & audio CD)
- Activity Book

Teaching notes & CLIL guidance: **www.oup.com/elt/teacher/readanddiscover**

Level / Subject Area	The World of Science & Technology	The Natural World	The World of Arts & Social Studies
1 — 300 headwords	• Eyes • Fruit • Trees • Wheels	• At the Beach • In the Sky • Wild Cats • Young Animals	• Art • Schools
2 — 450 headwords	• Electricity • Plastic • Sunny and Rainy • Your Body	• Camouflage • Earth • Farms • In the Mountains	• Cities • Jobs
3 — 600 headwords	• How We Make Products • Sound and Music • Super Structures • Your Five Senses	• Amazing Minibeasts • Animals in the Air • Life in Rainforests • Wonderful Water	• Festivals Around the World • Free Time Around the World
4 — 750 headwords	• All About Plants • How to Stay Healthy • Machines Then and Now • Why We Recycle	• All About Desert Life • All About Ocean Life • Animals at Night • Incredible Earth	• Animals in Art • Wonders of the Past
5 — 900 headwords	• Materials to Products • Medicine Then and Now • Transportation Then and Now • Wild Weather	• All About Islands • Animal Life Cycles • Exploring Our World • Great Migrations	• Homes Around the World • Our World in Art
6 — 1,050 headwords	• Cells and Microbes • Clothes Then and Now • Incredible Energy • Your Amazing Body	• All About Space • Caring for Our Planet • Earth Then and Now • Wonderful Ecosystems	• Food Around the World • Helping Around the World